MONKEY

by CAROLINE ARNOLD
Photographs by
RICHARD HEWETT

MORROW JUNIOR BOOKS • New York

The text type is 14-point Berkeley Old Style Medium.

Printed in Singapore at Tien Wah Press.
1 2 3 4 5 6 7 8 9 10
Library of Congress Cataloging-in-Publication Data. Arnold, Caroline. Monkey / Caroline Arnold ; photographs by Richard Hewett.   p.   cm.   Summary: Describes the physical characteristics, habits, behavior, natural environment, and zoo life of the red-crowned mangabey monkey.   ISBN 0-688-11342-7 (trade).—ISBN 0-688-11343-5 (library)   1. Red-crowned mangabey—Juvenile literature. [1. Red-crowned mangabey. 2. Monkeys.] I. Hewett, Richard, ill. II. Title. QL737.P93A76 1993 599.8′2—dc20   92-31095 CIP AC

ACKNOWLEDGMENTS

We are thankful for all the help we received on this project from the Los Angeles Zoo. We are especially grateful to June Bottcher, Special Programs Assistant; Jennie McNary, Senior Animal Keeper; and Robin Noll and Kelley Walsh, Animal Keepers, for their cheerful cooperation and willingness to answer our questions. We also thank Bob Barnes, Curator of Mammals, Los Angeles Zoo; Dr. Peter Waser, Purdue University; and Dr. John Oates, Hunter College, for their expert advice. And, as always, we thank our editor, Andrea Curley, for her continued enthusiastic support.

Leaping lightly on long, strong limbs, the young monkey jumped onto a fallen log. Although he was not yet fully grown, one-year-old Little Dude was nearly as agile as the older monkeys in his group. Always curious, he leaned forward to see what his mother had found. In her hands was a juicy slice of apple, one of Little Dude's favorite foods. She broke off a piece and gave it to him. Now he could have a taste, too.

Little Dude and his mother are a kind of monkey called the red-crowned mangabey. Together with three others of their species, they live in an enclosure at the Los Angeles Zoo in California. The keepers know each of the monkeys well and have given them names. In addition to Little Dude and his mother, Red, their group includes two adult females, Tip and Stub, and one adult male named Guy.

Although they are far from their native home in the coastal rain forests of West Africa, the group of red-crowned mangabeys at the zoo are comfortable and receive good care from the zoo staff. In their spacious enclosure the monkeys have ropes and poles for climbing, ledges and platforms for resting, and plenty of food and water.

Monkeys are always one of the most popular animals at zoos. Their lively behavior and obvious intelligence make them both fun and interesting to watch. In their natural habitat, most monkeys are difficult to study. They move quickly and can barely be seen when they are in the treetops or behind shrubbery. But by observing them in zoos we can learn more about them and better understand how their behavior and physical characteristics help them to live in their natural environment.

One reason that monkeys are so fascinating is the wide variety of ways that different species look and behave. If you have the chance to observe other monkey species at a zoo or animal park, try to see how they resemble or differ from red-crowned mangabeys. Red-crowned mangabeys are similar in many ways to other monkeys, especially to those that are closely related to them. However, the details of their life-style are unique to their species.

The red-crowned mangabey is a large long-tailed monkey with a long muzzle, slender body, and long limbs. Its most distinctive feature is the cap of bright russet fur on top of the head. The short, thick fur on the monkey's body is dark gray on its back and legs and white on its chest and belly. Its tail is gray, with a tuft of white hair at the end. Because of the collar, or ring, created by its white cheeks and the white patch of fur on the back of its neck, this species is also sometimes called the white-collared mangabey. Except for the light-colored skin above its eyes, the skin of the red-crowned mangabey is black.

The scientific name for the red-crowned mangabey is *Cercocebus torquatus torquatus*. This comes from Greek and Latin words meaning "twisted monkey tail." A special characteristic of the red-crowned mangabey is that it usually carries its tail up and curved over its back when walking. By raising or lowering the tail or by tapping its head with the tip of the tail, the monkey can convey signals to other members of its group.

In the wild, the red-crowned mangabey lives in Africa from Nigeria in the west to the Zaire (formerly the Congo) River in the east. It spends most of its time in rain forests and swamplands, moving constantly in search of food. Some red-crowned mangabeys live in national parks or forest reserves. However, the numbers of those that do not live in protected areas are shrinking because their forest habitat is being destroyed for logging and agriculture. Because places to live and sources of food are disappearing, the red-crowned mangabey is in danger of extinction.

Monkeys are a diverse group of animals with more than 100 different species, each uniquely adapted to its own habitat and life-style. Monkeys are found all over the world, and they range in size from the tiny 6-inch- (15.5-centimeter) long pygmy marmoset from South America, to the 2-foot- (.61-meter) long, 165-pound- (75-kilogram) baboon of the African plains. Most monkeys are found in places where the climate is warm—usually in tropical rain forests—although some, such as the Japanese macaque, live where winters are cold and snowy. In the rain forests where red-crowned mangabeys are found, it is warm and humid year round, and the seasons alternate between rainy and dry periods.

When scientists classify animals, they put closely related species in a group called a genus. (The plural form of "genus" is "genera.") Similar genera are placed in larger groups called families. The monkeys are divided into two large families, the Old World and the New World monkeys. Mangabeys are one genus in the family of Old World monkeys. There are about a dozen species of mangabeys, and they all live in Central or West Africa. (The exact number of species varies because scientists do not all agree about how some animals should be classified.)

All Old World monkeys live in either Africa or Asia. They include the macaques, baboons, mandrills, guenons, langur, and colobus monkeys and total about 58 species. More than 70 species

De Brazza's guenon (above)
and the black-and-white colobus (below)
are Old World monkeys from Africa.

of New World monkeys live in the Americas. They include the tamarins, marmosets, squirrel, woolly, capuchin, and howler monkeys. One difference between the two groups of monkeys is the tail. Many of the New World species have *prehensile* (or grasping) *tails*: In other words, they are able to use their tails much like a hand to hold on to things. The Old World monkeys cannot do this, although some species, such as the mangabeys, do hold on to branches loosely with their tails to steady themselves when climbing. Another difference between the two groups is the nostrils. Old World monkeys have nostrils that are close together and point downward. The New World monkeys have flat noses with widely spaced nostrils pointing to the side.

The woolly monkey is a New World species from South America.

All monkeys belong to a larger animal group called primates. Humans and apes are primates, too. Most primates have five fingers or toes on each hand or foot, which are covered by hard nails at the tips. In most species the thumb and big toe are opposite the other fingers or toes. This positioning enables the animal to grasp and hold on to objects, a skill that is particularly helpful to creatures that live in trees and use their hands and feet for climbing. The ability to grasp is also useful for picking up and holding on to food and other objects and for grooming.

Most primates also have eyes that face forward. This allows the animal to better judge the distance of objects. (Try closing one eye and you will discover how much more difficult it is to tell how far away something is than when you can see it with two eyes.) The ability to judge distances, or depth perception, is important for treetop living. When moving among branches, a mistake in judgment could mean a dangerous fall.

While other species of mangabeys live mainly in trees, the red-crowned mangabeys spend much of their life on the ground. Even when they are frightened, they usually run along the ground rather than escape through the trees. Nevertheless, they climb easily and often scamper up vines or branches to look for food or to find places to sleep or hide. Strong thigh muscles give mangabeys tremendous leaping power, and they can easily jump 12 to 19 feet (3.7 to 5.8 meters). At the zoo, Little Dude was an expert at jumping and swinging on the ropes and branches of the enclosure. He had developed a good sense of balance and coordination when he was still a baby.

Most primates live in social groups in which members regularly interact with one another and share food and other common resources. With monkeys, the social group can vary in size from a few animals to more than a hundred. In the wild, red-crowned mangabeys usually form groups composed of fourteen to twenty-three monkeys.

The way a primate social group is organized varies from species to species. Within all monkey groups, however, each animal has a particular rank, or standing. Higher-ranking monkeys play the dominant roles. They assert their dominance by chasing, fighting, and biting lower-ranking members of the group. High-ranking monkeys have the first choice of food, the best resting places, and in the case of males, the most

opportunities to mate. The leaders of a monkey group are usually one or more adult males because they are the biggest and strongest. At the zoo, Guy is the highest-ranking animal in the red-crowned mangabey group.

A young monkey's rank within its social group is determined at birth by the position of its mother. Because Red was the highest-ranking female in the red-crowned mangabey group at the zoo,

Little Dude shared in her high status. An individual's rank in the group can change as membership in the group changes (for instance, as animals leave or die), or as he or she grows stronger and fights the higher-ranked members for a more dominant position.

High-ranking monkeys receive the most grooming and also have their pick of grooming partners. Grooming one another's fur is a common activity of monkeys and apes. Using both hands and teeth, a monkey searches through its companion's fur for sticks, dirt, insects, and tangles. While grooming helps to keep the monkeys clean, it is also an important way for group members to establish and maintain relationships. Animals that are closely related or are of similar rank usually groom one another. For instance, a dominant male is groomed more often by a dominant female. This gives the female closer ties to the male and means that he is more likely to protect her if she is challenged by another member of the group.

A full-grown male red-crowned mangabey weighs between 19 and 27 pounds (8.6–12.3 kilograms) and can reach up to 26 inches (.67 meter) in length. The mangabey's tail is usually slightly longer than the length of its body. Male mangabeys reach their full size when they are five or six years old. Males are able to mate from the time they are three or four years old. Even though young males get an occasional chance to mate, dominant animals usually do most of the breeding. In a red-crowned mangabey group, the dominant male is usually at least seven years old.

As a young male matures, he must fight with older males in his group for the opportunity to mate. In the wild, a young male sometimes leaves his mother's social group when he becomes an adult. He may join another group and fight for a dominant position there. Or he may try to take a young female from his own or another group and start his own social group. When Little Dude becomes old enough to mate, he will probably go to another zoo.

The dominant male is responsible for keeping peace among the members of his group and for defending the group against outside threats. In the wild, he prevents the females from straying and other males from intruding. Although the dominant male does not usually help take care of the infants in his group, he does protect the mothers and their babies. As the young monkeys grow up, he sometimes plays with them, allowing them to climb on him or to swing on his tail. At the zoo, Little Dude and Guy sometimes played chasing games with each other.

Female red-crowned mangabey.

Female red-crowned mangabeys have the same coloring as males but they are somewhat smaller. An adult female is between 16 and 22 inches (.41 to .56 meter) in length and weighs about 11 pounds (5 kilograms). In the wild, female red-crowned mangabeys usually remain with their mother's group for their whole lives.

A female mangabey is able to mate for the first time when she is about three and a half to four years old. When she is ready to mate, the skin on her rump swells and becomes dark pink. After mating, she is pregnant for about seven months. The round belly of Tip, one of the females in the zoo enclosure, showed that she would soon give birth. Then Little Dude would no longer be the youngest monkey in the group.

Because the mother mangabey cares for her youngster for a year or more, she usually has a new baby only every year and a half to two years. In most cases, monkeys give birth to just one baby at a time. Although twins are occasionally born, it is hard for an active mother to care for two clinging infants.

One morning Little Dude woke up to the sound of an infant monkey calling to its mother. Tip's baby had been born during the night and her mother had already licked her clean. The little monkey, a female, snuggled close to her mother, but her wide eyes peered all around her. The keepers decided to name the new monkey Kitty.

At birth a mangabey weighs about 23 ounces (657.1 grams) and is about 7 inches (17.9 centimeters) long. The skin on Kitty's face, ears, hands, and feet was light pink, and her body was covered by a thin coat of fine-textured hair. When she is about eight weeks old, she will begin to get the heavier coat and darker skin of the older mangabeys.

Little Dude and the other monkeys were curious about the new baby and tried to get close to see it. At first, Tip protected her infant and turned away whenever the other mangabeys came near her, but after a few days she allowed them to touch Kitty and even groom her a little.

Like many other primate newborns, a baby red-crowned mangabey instinctively uses its hands and feet to grasp the fur on its mother's belly. There it clings tight, pressed close to her warm body. When hanging upside down, the baby sometimes puts its tail through its mother's legs and wraps the end of it around her leg or the base of her tail for extra support.

A newborn mangabey is stronger and more developed than a human baby. It can hold up its head, sit for short periods, and even crawl short distances. For the next few months, however, Tip will carry her baby.

As with other mammals, milk is a baby monkey's first food. Tip held Kitty close to her body, and whenever the infant became hungry, she could drink from one of the two nipples on her mother's chest. When Kitty is three to four months old, she will begin to nibble on solid food. Although one-year-old Little Dude was quite independent and could eat most foods, he still liked to nurse occasionally, too. Red will probably allow him to do this until her next baby is born.

Red-crowned mangabeys are vegetarians, and in the wild they feed mainly on fruits and nuts. In some places they share their forest habitat with another type of monkey called guenons. But the guenons live mainly in the upper branches of the trees, and the mangabeys spend more of their time on or near the ground. Therefore, each species eats only certain kinds of food, and so there is usually enough for everyone.

Although the red-crowned mangabeys feed mostly in forests, they occasionally raid farmers' fields and gardens. (They are particularly fond of rice, corn, and cacao beans.) In some places they are hunted by farmers who consider them a serious pest.

At the zoo, the monkeys are given a varied diet that includes fruit, green and yellow vegetables, peanuts, and monkey chow. The keepers usually scatter the food in several parts of the enclosure. This prevents conflicts and also allows the monkeys to search for and select their food, much as they would out in the wild.

A red-crowned mangabey has openings on the inside of its lower lips that go to deep pouches in its cheeks. If the monkey is in a hurry or is threatened with danger, it can stuff coarsely chewed food into these pockets. Then, when it has found a safe place to eat, the monkey uses the back of its hand to push the food up and out of the pouches and into its mouth. The food is then chewed thoroughly and swallowed.

The thirty-two teeth of a red-crowned mangabey are well suited to a varied diet. In the front, a mangabey has eight sharp incisors, four each in the upper and lower jaws. It uses its incisors to cut into tough foods such as palm nuts. Pointed canine teeth on either side of the incisors are good for ripping and tearing. In males, the canine teeth are larger and longer than in females and are used when fighting. On each side at the back of the mouth are flat premolar and molar teeth that are good for grinding and chewing. The mangabey uses its strong teeth to peel fruit, crack nuts and seeds, and chew the fibrous plant foods in its diet.

Although monkeys get much of the moisture they need from their food, they also need water to drink. In the wild, red-crowned mangabeys never travel far from the rivers or lakes that provide their drinking water. At the zoo, the keepers fill the small pool in the red-crowned mangabey enclosure with fresh water daily. Little Dude soon discovered that splashing at the edge of the pool during hot weather was a good way to keep cool. Sometimes the mangabeys also used the water in their pool to wash pieces of food.

Animals that live in groups can help one another find food, water, and other things they need to live. Another advantage of living in a group is that there are more eyes and ears to watch and listen for danger. When one of the monkeys in the group notices a predator, it signals with loud cries to the others to be alert. (In addition to people, who sometimes hunt monkeys for food or as pests, natural predators of mangabeys include leopards and eagles.)

One of the most important ways that monkeys communicate with one another is by sound. Most monkeys are noisy, and even at the zoo you know when you are near a monkey group just from hearing their whoops, calls, barks, and grunts. In the wild, monkeys may not be able to see one another in the treetops or in dense vegetation, but they can hear the others' calls. Certain very loud sounds warn other monkey groups not to come near. Other sounds help keep the group together as its members move from one place to another. Sounds are also used to express anger, distress, or pleasure. Facial expressions and body postures are also ways that monkeys communicate with one another.

The red-crowned mangabeys, and the closely related sooty and white-crowned mangabeys, have another way of communicating. When they close their eyes the white lids stand out against their dark faces. They sometimes send signals to one another by blinking their eyes rapidly to reveal these white patches.

Every day, the zookeepers clean the red-crowned mangabeys' enclosure and check to make sure that all the animals seem healthy. The monkeys have learned to trust the keepers and usually come over for a special treat. Mangabeys are noted for their curiosity and can be quite friendly, but they are never completely tame. Although the zookeepers have a good relationship with the mangabeys, they are always careful. All monkeys are wild animals and can be dangerous if they become frightened or angry. Even though pet stores sometimes sell monkeys, they do not usually make good household pets.

In the wild, one of the main activities for monkeys is finding food to eat. When food is provided, as it is for animals in captivity, life can be boring. To make the monkeys' days more interesting and more like life in the wild, the keepers at the zoo give them occasional treats. A coconut or pumpkin, for instance, is both a toy and something good to eat. As the animals work to break these items apart and to extract the parts that are good to eat, they are practicing skills that would help them survive in the wild.

In the summer, children who attend zoo camp stuff pinecones with nuts and peanut butter as one of their activities. Then they watch as the monkeys search the pinecones and discover their treats. The animals seem to enjoy the challenge of removing the nuts from the cracks in the pinecones, and at the same time they get extra nutrition.

Sometimes Little Dude chased or wrestled with the older mangabeys, but usually he played by himself or with his mother. Like other young monkeys, Little Dude was curious about his surroundings and was constantly exploring. One day he discovered a large stick in the enclosure. At first he tasted it to see if it might be good to eat. Eventually he found that by pushing the stick against the ground he could use it as a vaulting pole to do tricks and somersaults. Although it seemed as if Little Dude played just for fun, the exercise helped him to strengthen his muscles, sharpen his reflexes, and develop his coordination. For young animals both in captivity and in the wild, these kinds of play activities help prepare them for adult life.

When a red-crowned mangabey is about six weeks old, it begins to leave its mother for short periods. In a group where there are other youngsters, it spends much of its time playing and exploring with them. Soon Kitty will be old enough to begin exploring. Then Little Dude will have a playmate.

As a young monkey grows up in a social group, it learns how to cope with its world both from its mother and from other members of its group. They protect and care for the youngster while it learns how to find food, move about, and take care of itself. Gradually it becomes an expert at recognizing and manipulating objects, learns to react quickly to new situations, and begins to establish relationships that may last a lifetime. We do not know how long red-crowned mangabeys live in the wild, but in captivity, they can live for twenty years or more as long as they receive nutritious food and good care.

In 1562, a Flemish artist named Pieter Brueghel painted a picture of two red-crowned mangabeys sitting on a windowsill that overlooked a harbor in the Netherlands. The monkeys had been brought back by a sea captain from the African coast. This is one of our earliest records of red-crowned mangabeys in captivity. Today many people are familiar with red-crowned mangabeys because they can watch them at zoos.

As we learn more about the many different ways that monkeys live and interact with one another, both in captivity and in the wild, we gain insights into the meaning of their behaviors. Also, because the bodies of monkeys are similar in many ways to humans, they have been useful for research into the causes and cures of some human diseases. Monkeys like Little Dude and the other red-crowned mangabeys in his group help us to appreciate the enormous diversity of life as well as the variety of adaptations that enable each species to survive.

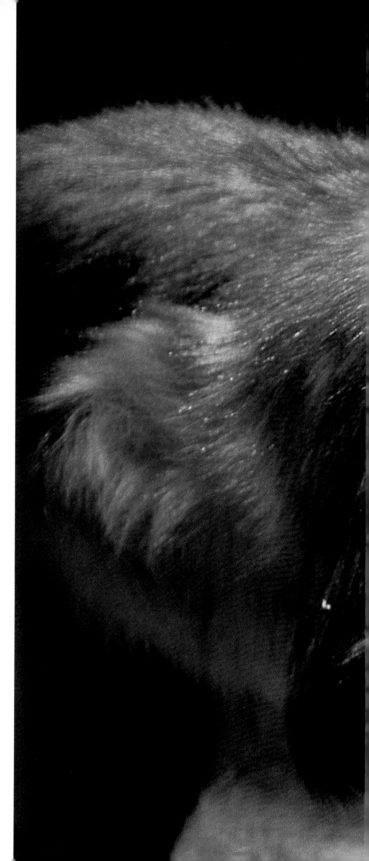

INDEX